ESSENTIAL
shakes

Caroline Westmore

Photography by Peter Wakeman
Design by Sam Grimmer

HINKLER
BOOKS

HINKLER
BOOKS

Dingley Victoria Australia

Copyright © Hinkler Books Pty. Ltd. 2001

First printed 2002

Creative director: Sam Grimmer

ISBN 1 86515 395 8

Printed and bound in China

contents Introduction   4

Introduction

This book contains a wide variety of recipes ranging from traditional shakes through to sodas, smoothies and even fresh ices. Not all the drinks are dairy based, but every one has a delicious flavour, and is able to be adapted to suit individual tastes. Whether your aim is to relax your body with a dairy shake, feel refreshed with a soda, replenish nutrients by drinking a smoothie or cool down with an ice, there is a drink in this book to suit your needs. The recipes have been divided into four sections.

smoothies

Smoothies could well be said to offer a meal in a glass. The more traditional yogurt smoothies will aid your digestion, while others (such as Big Breakfast) can get your system in motion for the day ahead. Deliciously fruity combinations (such as the Black Forest and Mango Calypso) will give you the energy required if you happen to miss a meal or are in too much of a hurry to sit down and eat.

shakes

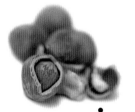

Shakes, of course, encompass many traditional-style recipes for dairy-based drinks. Shakes are rich and smooth, full of ice cream, toppings and flavours such as chocolate, coffee and vanilla. Not only delicious, these shakes are also great sources of calcium and energy, and thus the perfect snack for after school or between meals.

ices

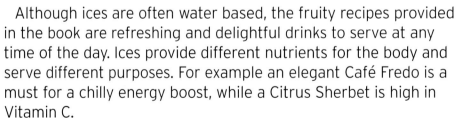

Although ices are often water based, the fruity recipes provided in the book are refreshing and delightful drinks to serve at any time of the day. Ices provide different nutrients for the body and serve different purposes. For example an elegant Café Fredo is a must for a chilly energy boost, while a Citrus Sherbet is high in Vitamin C.

sodas

Sodas are less filling than shakes, although equally tempting. From the traditional ice cream soda, to the more relaxed style spritzers, the soda section has a variety of drinks for many occasions. These drinks can be very refreshing and relaxing.

equipment

The essential piece of equipment needed to make the recipes in this book is an efficient blender. It must be strong enough to blend ice, so make sure that your blender has a metal blade and powerful motor. You should also have various mixing spoons and measures, a strong ice cream scoop and a citrus juicer (such as a hand juicer or citrus reamer). A zester is a handy tool as it removes just the coloured zest from the peel and not the bitter white pith. To add variety and flair you may also choose to invest in a range of interesting glassware which can be used to serve the drinks.

Do not be afraid to alter the recipes according to your taste, or according to the availability and seasonality of some ingredients. You can always substitute frozen berries for fresh ones, or canned fruit when fresh fruit is out of season. You may also wish to vary your drinking habits according to the time of year, for example ices may be your preferred drink during summer. Versatile and easy to make, these drinks are there to be enjoyed all year round.

CONVERSION INDEX		
Remember to carefully follow either metric or imperial weights and measures. Never use a combination of both, as they are not exact equivalents.	1 teaspoon = 5 ml	
	1 cup (250 ml)	
	METRIC	IMPERIAL
	30 ml	1 fl oz
	250 ml	8 fl oz
	30 g	1 oz
	250 g	8 oz
	500 g	16 oz (1 lb)

Black Forest

425 g canned pitted black cherries
500 ml (16 fl oz) milk
4 scoops vanilla ice cream or vanilla frozen yoghurt
30 ml (1 fl oz) chocolate topping
fresh cherries

Place all the ingredients including the cherry juice in a blender and blend on high speed until thick and creamy. Serve garnished with fresh cherries if desired.

Makes about 1 litre (32 fl oz)

blac

k forest

ode to

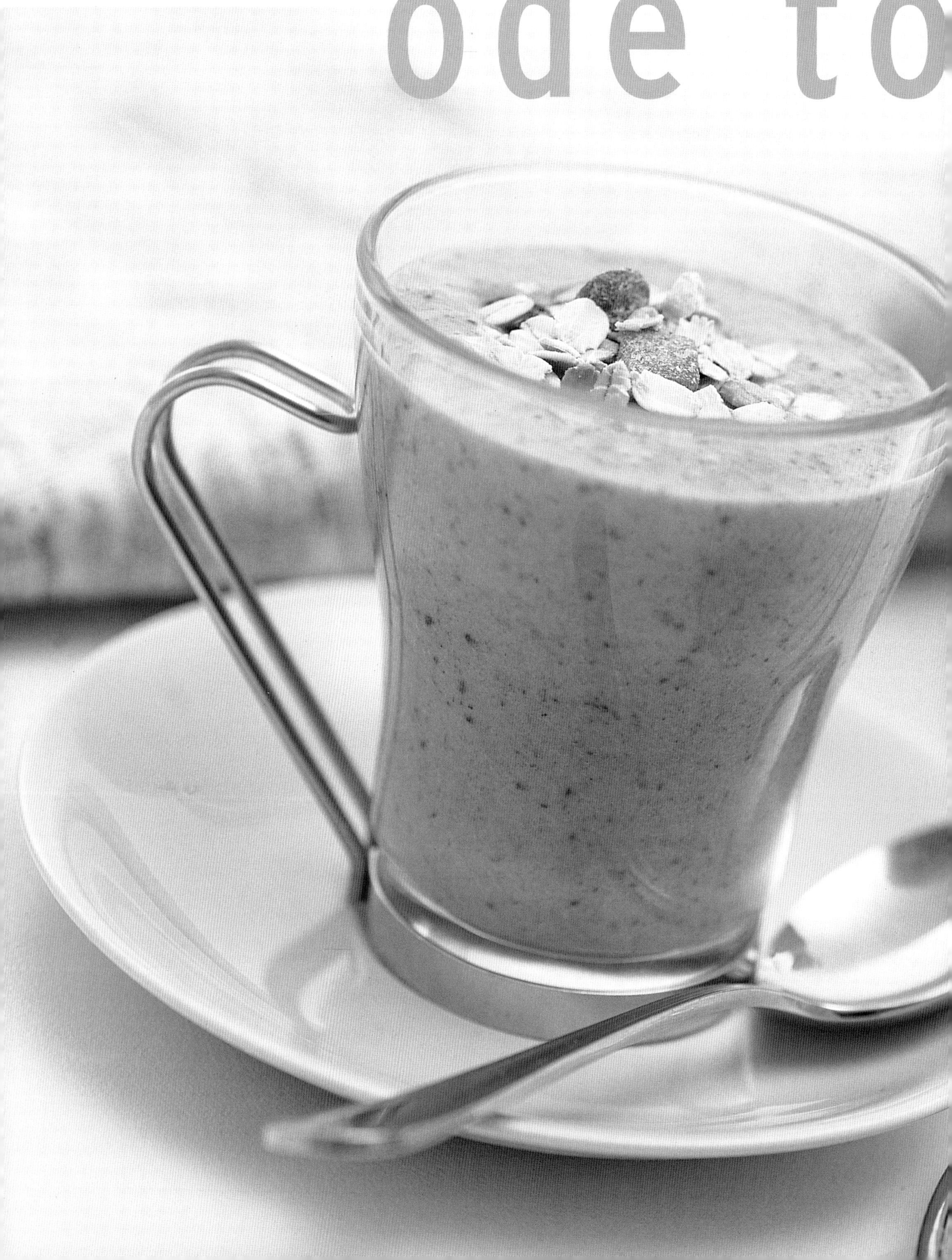

the prune

Ode to the Prune

4 stoned prunes
250 ml (8 fl oz) boiling water
1 large ripe banana
250 ml (8 fl oz) apple or pear juice
2 scoops frozen vanilla yoghurt or ice cream
2 tablespoons muesli

Soak the prunes in the boiling water. Let the prunes cool in the water, then place both the prunes and the water, the peeled banana, juice and frozen yoghurt or ice cream in a blender. Blend until smooth and top with muesli.

Makes about 1 litre (32 fl oz)

Lassi Come Home

1 mango
1 soft peach
½ cup natural yoghurt
250 ml (8 fl oz) water, chilled
1 cup ice cubes
1 teaspoon honey

Remove the skin and stone from the mango and the peach. Place all the ingredients in a blender and blend on high speed until smooth. Stir through honey and serve.

Makes about 750 ml (24 fl oz)

Lassi is a traditional Indian drink made from a base of yoghurt and water with other ingredients added for flavour or effect.

me home

Violet Illusion

825 g (26 oz) canned dark plums in syrup
200 ml (6 fl oz) apple juice
2 scoops vanilla ice cream

Remove the stones from the plums. Place the plums and syrup in a blender with the apple juice and ice cream and blend until smooth.

Makes about 1 litre (32 fl oz)

viol

et illusion

banana
na na

Banana Nut
Na Na Na Na Na

1 ripe banana
2 scoops vanilla soy ice confection
2 cups soy drink
nutmeg

Place all the ingredients except the nutmeg in a blender and blend until smooth. Pour the mixture into glasses and sprinkle with nutmeg.

Makes about 750 ml (24 fl oz)

Crushed Velvet

200 g (6 oz) berry yoghurt
30 ml (1 fl oz) blackcurrant cordial
250 g (8 oz) fresh or frozen
    blackcurrants or blackberries
250 ml (8 fl oz) milk
$\frac{1}{3}$ cup crushed ice

Place all the ingredients in a blender and blend
until the berries and ice are finely crushed.

Makes about 750 ml (24 fl oz)

crushed

elvet

eakfast

Big Breakfast

**1 ripe banana
1 shot espresso, chilled
250 ml (8 fl oz) milk
200 g (6 oz) vanilla yoghurt
1 teaspoon honey
2 teaspoons wheatgerm**

Peel the banana and combine all the ingredients in a blender. Blend until smooth.

Makes about 500 ml (16 fl oz)

This breakfast provides you with essential carbohydrates, fibre, energy and calcium plus a good shot of caffeine to really break your fast.

bullwin

Bullwinkle

30 g (1 oz) chocolate topping
50 g (1³/₄ oz) hazelnut meal
1 ripe banana
1 scoop chocolate ice cream
250 ml (8 fl oz) milk

Dip the rim of the glass in chocolate topping, then into the hazelnut meal. Peel the banana. Blend the ice cream, milk, banana and the remaining hazelnut meal in a blender until smooth.

Makes about 500 ml (16 fl oz)

kle

You Sexy Thing

30 ml (1 fl oz) chocolate topping
250 ml (8 fl oz) milk
marshmallows

Drizzle the chocolate topping down the inside of a tall glass. Heat the milk until hot (not boiling) and pour into the glass. Serve with marshmallows.

Makes about 250 ml (8 fl oz)

thing

happ

Happy Daze

30 ml (1 fl oz) caramel topping
1 scoop ice cream
250 ml (8 fl oz) milk
2 teaspoons malted milk powder

Combine all the ingredients in a blender and blend until smooth and frothy. Serve chilled.

Makes about 300 ml (10 fl oz)

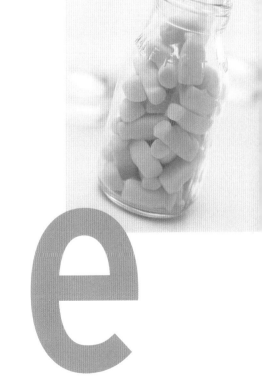

daze

monk

Monkey Business

4 teaspoons smooth peanut butter
1 ripe banana
250 ml (8 fl oz) pouring custard
500 ml (16 fl oz) skim milk
1 cup ice cubes
cinnamon

Place all the ingredients except cinnamon in a blender and blend until smooth. Pour the mixture into glasses and garnish with a sprinkle of cinnamon.

Makes about 1 litre (32 fl oz)

ey business

Liquid Melba

30 ml (1 fl oz) raspberry topping
425 g (14 fl oz) peaches in natural juice
3 scoops vanilla ice cream
4 coconut macaroons, crushed

Drizzle the raspberry topping into the base of four glasses. Blend the peaches with the peach juice and ice cream, pour the mixture into the glasses and top with the crushed coconut macaroons.

Makes about 650 ml (22 fl oz)

elba

vienna mo

Vienna Moon

2 shots of espresso coffee
1 teaspoon sugar
2 scoops vanilla or coffee ice cream
250 ml (8 fl oz) milk
cinnamon

Combine the hot coffee and sugar, then chill. Place the ice cream and milk in a blender, add the coffee mixture and blend until smooth. Pour the mixture into glasses and top with extra ice cream if desired, then sprinkle with cinnamon.

Makes about 500 ml (16 fl oz)

choc-full-

kryp

Choc-Full-o-Kryptonite

60 ml (2 fl oz) chocolate topping
2 drops peppermint essence
3 scoops vanilla ice cream
250 ml (8 fl oz) milk
1 teaspoon chocolate flakes

Pour half the chocolate topping around the inside of the glass. Place the remaining topping, the peppermint essence, two scoops of the ice cream and the milk into a blender and blend until smooth. To serve, place the third scoop of ice cream into a glass and top up with the mixture. Sprinkle with chocolate flakes.

Makes about 450 ml (14 fl oz)

tonite

Turkish Delight

1 lime
200 ml (7 fl oz) commercial cranberry juice
4 teaspoons rose water
1 cup crushed ice

Juice the lime then place the juice with the rest of the ingredients in a blender and blend until smooth.

Makes about 650 ml (22 fl oz)

turkish deli

ght

citrus

herbet

Citrus Sherbet

2 lemons
250 g (8 oz) sugar
250 ml (8 fl oz) water
1 orange
1 lime
lemon squash to taste

Juice the lemons and save the zest. Heat the sugar and water, stirring until the sugar is dissolved. Add the lemon juice and zest.
Place the mixture into a flat tray and freeze overnight. When the sherbet is frozen, break up any large ice crystals with a fork, then refreeze.

Juice the orange and lime. Scoop the sherbet into a glass and pour the orange and lime juice over it. Top up with lemon squash.

Makes 750 ml (24 fl oz) of sherbet

Snow Bunny

12 strawberries
1 orange
250 ml (8 fl oz) pineapple juice
1¹/₂ cups ice cubes

Hull the strawberries. Peel the orange and cut it into pieces. Place all the ingredients in a blender and blend until smooth.

Makes about 750 ml (24 fl oz)

W
nny

g i

Ginger Rogers

825 g (26 oz) canned pineapple pieces in natural juice
1¹/₂ cups ice cubes
ginger beer to taste

Blend the pineapple pieces including the natural juice and ice. Pour the mixture into glasses and top up with ginger beer.

Makes 1 litre (32 fl oz)

mocha
gr

anita

Mocha Granita

4 shots espresso coffee
60 ml (2 fl oz) rich chocolate topping
2 cups ice cubes

Combine all the ingredients in a blender and blend until thick and icy.

Makes about 500 ml (16 fl oz)

café

Café Fredo

6 shots espresso coffee
6 teaspoons sugar
1½ cups ice cubes

Combine the hot coffee and sugar, then chill. Place the coffee in a blender with the ice and blend until smooth, or alternately pour the sweetened coffee over the ice.

Makes 600 ml (20 fl oz)

redo

45

Glass Slipper

250 g (8 oz) raspberries and strawberries
100 ml (3 fl oz) milk
2 scoops vanilla ice cream
½ cup ice cubes

Hull the strawberries, then place the berries in a blender
with the milk, ice cream and ice. Blend until smooth.

Makes 500 ml (16 fl oz)

glass
slipp

er

lime sub

Lime Sub-Lime

¼ watermelon
1 lime
4 teaspoons lime cordial
1 cup ice cubes
500 ml (16 fl oz) lemon squash

Cut the watermelon into chunks and remove
the pips. Juice the lime. Place the watermelon
pieces in a blender with the lime juice, cordial
and ice. Blend until smooth, then top up with
the lemon squash and serve immediately.

Makes about 1 litre (32 fl oz)

lime

Royal Jelly

30 ml (1 fl oz) honey
30 ml (1 fl oz) lemon juice
250 ml (8 fl oz) dry ginger ale, chilled
lemon slices

Combine the honey with the lemon juice and stir until
the two liquids are mixed together. Top up with the dry
ginger ale and garnish with the lemon slices.

Makes about 310 ml (10 fl oz)

roya

1 TEA SPOON

jelly

van

illa
revival

Vanilla Revival

1 scoop vanilla ice cream
150 ml (5 fl oz) creamy soda, chilled
vanilla pod

Place the scoop of ice cream into a glass
and pour over the creamy soda. Stir the
drink with the vanilla pod, then serve.

Makes about 200 ml (6 fl oz)

Jungle Juice

500 ml (16 fl oz) pineapple juice
30 ml (1 fl oz) lime cordial
1¹/₂ cups ice cubes
2 scoops lemon sorbet

Place all the ingredients in a blender
and blend until smooth and icy.

Makes about 1 litre (32 fl oz)

jungle

juice

be

Berry Basic

1 scoop vanilla ice cream
150 ml (5 fl oz) raspberry soda
1/2 dozen fresh or frozen raspberries

Place the scoop of ice cream in a glass and top up slowly with raspberry soda. Serve immediately garnished with raspberries.

Makes 200 ml (6 fl oz)

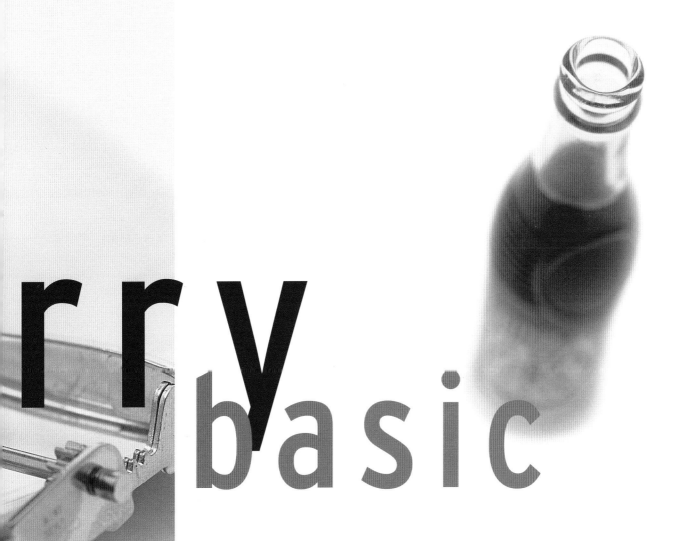

rry basic

Margi Fizz

1 orange
1 lime
³/₄ cup ice cubes
250 ml (8 fl oz) commercial cranberry juice
fresh or frozen raspberries or cranberries
tonic water to taste

Juice the orange and lime. Place the juices and ice in a blender with the cranberry juice and blend until smooth. Pour the mixture into four glasses, add the berries and top up with tonic water to taste.

Makes about 600 ml (20 fl oz)

margifi

59

cit

Citron Pressé

4 lemons
4 limes
500 ml (16 fl oz) soda water
sugar to taste

Juice the lemons and limes and save the zest. Add the zest and the juices to a jug and top up with the soda water. Mix well. Place sugar to taste in a glass with extra zest, then fill with Citron Pressé.

Makes about 600 ml (20 fl oz)

ron
pressé

In the pink

250 ml (8 fl oz) commercial cranberry juice
1 cup ice cubes
4 scoops berry sorbet
250 ml (8 fl oz) mineral water or lemon squash

Place the cranberry juice, ice cubes and berry sorbet into a blender and blend until smooth. Half fill serving glasses, then top up with mineral water or lemon squash.

Makes about 600 ml (20 fl oz)

This is also delicious with a dash of fresh pink grapefruit juice or freshly squeezed lemon juice.

in the p

ink

acknowledgments

The author would like to thank the following people and organisations for their help in preparing this book:
My assistant Jane and Peter the photographer for their hard work, affection and incredible sense of fun. Our mothers, Claire, Margi and Gwenda, to Linda and Kirsty at Kraft and Tami at McCormick for allowing me to raid their kitchen cupboards. Everyone at Albert Park Fruit Palace, especially Jason and Joe; Australian Hospitality Dinnerware for their beautiful glasses and plates; and Breville for their shiny new appliances. The adorable Sam for making the book so funky; Brigid for crossing my t's and dotting my i's so often and with good humour; Louise for taking the bull by the horns; and Steve and Tracey for conceiving the project.